An  of HOPE

Inspirational Stories and Devotionals

ISBN: 0-9656097-0-7

Unless otherwise specified, Scripture quotations are from the *Holy Bible: New International Version* ©1973, 1978, 1984, by International Bible Society.

Cover Photo: Superstock
Back Cover photo of Debbie Harned by Dana A. Morton

"Sermons We See" is from "Collected Verse of Edgar A. Guest," copyright © 1934. Reprinted with permission of Contempory Book, Inc. Chicago.

© 1997 by Anchor Ministries, Inc. All rights reserved. No portion of this book may be reporduced, stored, or transimitted by any means, mechanical, electronic, or otherwise, without the express written consent of the publisher.

Anchors of Hope

*Take hold of your anchor —
the cross with a smile,
And carry it with you
through every trial.*

*This life is a journey.
The Son lights our way.
Our paths are all different,
and yet, much the same.*

*To help one another
is part of God's plan.
So, love and encourage
and do what you can.*

*All hope is in Jesus,
and He is alive!
With Anchors of Hope
you can live, not just survive.*

Leigh A. Hutcherson

To Jesus, my Anchor,
    There is no storm too great nor a sprinkle too small that I don't need to call out your name.

To my Family and Friends,
    I dedicate this book to your love, support, and encouragement. May you realize the importance of your anchoring presence in my life.

Contents

Introduction 7
It's the Cross and a Smile 8
Time to Anchor 10

Laws of the Lighthouse
   Anchoring Hope Forever 11
   Anchors of Strength 25

Who Am I?
   Anchoring Hope in Knowing 29
   Anchors of Worth 43

Do You . . .?
   Anchoring Hope with Life 47
   Anchors of Action 57

Ways to Encourage
   Anchoring Hope through Courage 61
   Anchors of Support 75

Risk
   Anchoring Hope on the Edge 79
   Anchors of Security 91

Introduction

This book is designed to be used in two ways. One way is to provide inspirational stories of hope and encouragement. May the stories inspire you. Perhaps walk with you. Be encouraging to you in stormy times of your life. In our journey, it's important to know that our paths cross and look similar. Many times just knowing what God has done in other's lives gives us inspiration to continue our journey.

The second way to use this book is through the devotionals. These devotionals are designed to help you make and spend special one on one time with God. Let Him meet, change and mold you. May these devotionals encourage you to find your anchor points in Him and Him alone. They are laid out in five sets. Each set of devotionals stands on its own. Yet, they all lead to our Anchor of Hope in Jesus.

Have fun with this book, the stories and devotionals. God is more interested in your relationship with Him, rather than just a ritual.

It's the Cross and a Smile

Anchors - have you ever thought much about an anchor? Most of the time we see them either displayed in a museum, coming up over the side of a ship or resting at the front of a boat. Anchors, however, are incredibly important. Not only are they important to the person in charge of the ship, anchors are important to the persons on the ship.

So do you have to be a nautical person in order to enjoy anchors? I don't think so! It was once written about me that to look at me is to think I was Navy through and through. But my love and appreciation for anchors did not come by way of a branch of the United States Armed Services.

Anchors became real in my life because of the storms. Storms like we all have. Some big. Some little. All lead back however to the same point - the point to which you hold on in order to make it through. When you anchor your life to the cross of Christ, you will always find hope. Hope in another person cheering for you. Hope in an unexpected outcome. Hope in knowing you are not alone. Hope in living on, even when you think you cannot!

Anchors are simple to draw. Take a pen/pencil. First draw a cross—then at the bottom of the cross add a smile.

Pretty cool! Don't you think? It's not amazing however, that an anchor which appears so simple to draw is so rich in meaning. An anchor contains elements of encouragement and hope. It's the cross of Christ along with the smiles of His love. It's forever embraced by believers hanging on to Hope!

"We have this hope as an anchor for the soul, firm and secure." Hebrews 6:19 (N.I.V.)

The word "anchor" is only found three times in the Bible (New International Version). Two times were in reference to the actual item called an anchor. The other is the above verse. Yet, with such little reference, we know that the actual anchor has been around and useful for many years.

The word "hope" is found in the Bible 158 times (New International Version). Is this word important because it's in the Bible more? Let's hope not! But the number of times in the Bible does give help to remind us of the importance of this significant word.

Anchors of Hope—not necessarily words put together in the Bible, but thoughts put together in our hearts! Let's anchor to hope! Because, it's not what we tie our lives to— it's what we anchor our lives in. Anchor your life in the hope of Jesus Christ.

For I know the plans I have for you," declares the Lord, "plans to prosper you and not to harm you, plans to give you hope and a future."
Jeremiah 29:11

Time to Anchor

To find your "Anchors of Hope" in these devotionals, take each devotional and spend a special time with the Father. There are six in each section, five sections for a total of 30 devotionals.

✔ Find a special place - your place of peace and quiet.

✔ Make notes in this book and in your Bible. We cannot and do not always remember information - so write it down. Many devotionals will ask you to use the "Anchor Notes" sheet. That is the blank sheet on the opposite side of the devotional. It's blank for a reason.

These devotionals are written for you and God. I want your time and answers to be yours, not mine.

Anchor deep!

"Be still and know that I am God; . . ."
Psalm 46:10

Inspirational Stories and Devotionals

Laws of the Lighthouse

Anchoring Hope Forever

In these devotionals, you are challenged to write statements called "Laws of the Lighthouse". After searching your heart, and spending time with the Father, search out truths or statements of your own you call your "laws of the lighthouse."

You'll need them when the storms come. You'll need them when you're ship seems battered and about to go under.

As you discover your laws of the lighthouse, you'll find more strength for being anchored in hope.

"The Lord is my rock, my fortress and my deliverer; my God is my rock, in whom I take refuge."
Psalm 18:2

Anchor Notes

Inspirational Stories and Devotionals

Laws of the Lighthouse

When you think of the above title, what comes to your mind?

Laws are important!

law (lô) n.
1. A rule of conduct or procedure established by custom, agreement, or authority

Lighthouses are unique!

lighthouse n. Nautical.
A tall structure topped by a powerful light used as a beacon or signal to aid marine navigation.

In your mind, picture a lighthouse:
When you touch it, how does it feel?

How does the air around this lighthouse smell?

How does this lighthouse function?

Check out Psalm 18:1 - 3.
These verses describe a "law of the lighthouse". In them hold a never-ending, forever guiding truth. As you read the scripture againask God to help you find *your* law of truth in these scriptures.
Write out your first "Law of the Lighthouse"

_____

_____

 **Anchor Notes**

....

....

....

....

....

....

Laws of the Lighthouse

One of my favorite "Laws of the Lighthouse" found in Max Lucado's book, *In the Eye of the Storm*, is:

> ## "Succeed at home."

What a unique thought—especially in today's society?
Think of your home—when you think of success—what comes to mind?

When was the last time you thought about being a success with your family or in your family? Don't have to because they are just supposed to love us anyway! (oops—we're only suppose to think that—not say it!)

Check out Joshua 24:15. What message do you get from that verse?

Anchors of Hope

With that message and in light of God's truths about our homes and families, what "law of the lighthouse" can you write about this important area of your life?

Laws of the Lighthouse

There are many functions of a lighthouse.

First—it warns of impending danger—the light of a lighthouse is a warning. It not only shines upon the ship, but it also shines upon the danger.

In Ephesians 4:17—32 Paul brings to light impending danger. Read these verses and list the "dangers" brought to light in your life:

_____

_____

The New International Version of the Bible even subtitles those verses, "Living as Children of the Light".

What happens to you when you don't take heed of the lighthouse's warning concerning these issues?

_____

_____

We will and many times do crash and wreck if we don't pay attention to the lighthouse's warning.

From those verses and God's leadership in your life—write your second "law of the lighthouse"

_____

_____

Anchor Notes

Inspirational Stories and Devotionals

Laws of the Lighthouse

When was the last time you felt like you were in a fog?

What makes up your "fog"?

_____

_____

There are times in each of our lives where any number of things could and do cause us to go into a fog. We're not sure if we are going to run into trouble because we can't see through.

>Remember in times of fog—
>Psalm 30:5
>Isaiah 40:31
>2 Cor. 1:3-4
>Rom. 8:38-39
>Psalm 147:3
>1 Peter 5:6 -7

What message of light do you find in these scriptures?

_____

_____

_____

Which scripture passage is especially helpful to you today? Why?

From scripture and talking with God today, write your "law of the lighthouse" concerning fog.

Anchor Notes

Inspirational Stories and Devotionals

Laws of the Lighthouse

Take a minute and look back over the four "Laws of the Lighthouse" you've already written. List them below.

▮ _____

▮ _____

▮ _____

▮ _____

Great job!
(this book has been electronically wired to know whether or not you have written anything)

Anchors of Hope

As you look back over the important statements that you've come to realize are so important to you, can you think of others you consider "laws of the lighthouse"?

It may take a while to think of other "Laws of the Lighthouse." I don't think you will be sorry because you took the time. These statements will be important or have been important to you from this day forward.

Don't forget to give God thanks for these laws. Be sure to allow His loving protection to guide you. Remember where the source of the light comes from!

Laws of the Lighthouse

In doing this devotional, if you had the C.D. *My Utmost for His Highest*, it would be to your advantage to hear this song: "Shine On Me."

Question—Of all the parts that make up a lighthouse, which is the most important?

A Lighthouse is not a Lighthouse without the light.

The Psalmist stated:
"Let the light of your face shine upon us, O Lord."

Can you feel that statement?

Can you understand what the Psalmist was asking of God? Will you, O God give us the light? Will all that you are—come and shine (personally) on us?

The song, "Shine On Me" is an incredible song. The Christian group, Phillips, Craig & Dean sing it on the C.D. The words are as follows:

> "Lord, let your light
> Light of Your face
> Shine on us
> That we may be saved
> That we may have life
> To find our way in the darkest night
> Let Your light shine on us"

(if you have the song, take a few minutes and let this beautiful song minister to you)

In light of the source of the lighthouse, and all that you've experienced during this devotional, write one last law of the lighthouse—

_____

_____

 # Anchor Notes

Anchors of Strength

We write statements that constitute our personal "Laws of the Lighthouse". Statements we count on and live with daily. We ask God to give us the strength—to anchor to His teachings. To have the strength to anchor with ourselves and friends.

Then Jesus decides to teach us and all those on that mountain in Matthew about the importance of our light shining. When Jesus shared this statement, He wasn't referring to us and lighthouses, but He could have. The light which should shine in a lighthouse should also shine in us. What hope we have in that fact. Because of Him, we are lights of worth. We shine and give guidance and light to others!

"You are the light of the world. A city on a hill cannot be hidden. Neither do people light a lamp and put it under a bowl. Instead they put it on its stand, and it gives light to everyone in the house. In the same way, let your light so shine before men, that they may see your good deeds and praise your Father in heaven." (Matthew 5:14-16)

Hiring people to work with you is not always the easiest of things. As their boss, there comes such things as expectations, deadlines, and responsibilities. When your employee lets up, you have to kick in and pick up the slack. Not always when you want or need to, but the buck stops with you. Hopefully!

I hired someone once. Because this young man was different, it stretched those around me to accept this young man at first. To some he was different but to me he was great.

He brought to our task some unique qualities, gifts and

perspectives. Although it was not in his job description to love all those around him, he did. His job seemed less than important compared to the way he loved those around him, especially those who lacked such love.

In our job, we dealt with lots of children. Children of all ages. Children who's stories and lives were just beginning. Some children who's stories already had lots of chapters. Chapters with some good, some with pain.

To one little guy, my employee became an anchor of strength, a lighthouse of hope. When these two lives came together, the needs of one child and the strength of a young man became the example of God's guiding strength and love.

How do I know this? I witnessed it. Not only through out the beginning stages of their friendship, but also at the end. It was a Kodak moment I remember the most. No film, however, could ever replace what I watched and is printed on my heart.

After several years of working with us, my employee decided to leave our job. His life calling was out beyond our walls. It was his time to fly and began more of his journey. Saying good bye was not something he wanted to do, but I felt it necessary for those whose lives he had touched. So I did what any good boss would do—throw a farewell surprise party.

At the party, all the children had their chance to give back a small gift of their love to this neat young man. It was wonderful to watch them bring joy and tons of smiles to my now leaving employee.

The party had ended and most of us were heading out the door. All except my employee and his young admirer. As I walked out the door, I failed to hear the two of them talking. The basketball they were sharing was now silent. I turned and captured what the "Anchor of Strength" is all about. The young admirer could not hold it any more. Tears streamed down both of their faces, actually all three of our faces. Liquid love. Flowing from my employee—a person who had loved unconditionally. A person who had taught his little friend that in Christ there is something to Anchor your life within. A man who taught a young boy that there are lighthouses along life's way to keep you from hitting the dangerous shores.

I walked out anchored. Anchored in the strength that each of us have people, things, beliefs, that God wants us to hold on too. These strengths are our lighthouses. The laws of the lighthouse teach us that God uses these strengths to help us make it through the journey.

> *"Be strong in the Lord and in his mighty power."*
> *Ephesians 6:10*

You are a lighthouse to others because of "whose" you are! Not because of something that you've earned or done, just by your relationship. So when you ask the question, now who am I in all this? Remember to anchor your hope in the strength of His Light!

"I am the light of the world. Whoever follows me will never walk in darkness, but will have the light of life."
John 8:12

" For God, who said "Let light shine out of darkness," made his light shine in our hearts to give us the light of the knowledge of the glory of God in the face of Christ."
2 Corinthians 4:6

Letters of Hope

Take a minute. Write a prayer. Share a word of thanks to God for His strength.

_____

_____

_____

_____

_____

_____

_____

_____

_____

_____

_____

_____

Who Am I?

Anchoring Hope in Knowing

Philosophers, theologians, people throughout the ages have all asked the question, "Who am I?" So to say that this question is a creative, original one, worthy of devotionals—is a bit misleading. It is worthy of spending time with God, however, and finding out who you are to Him!

Each of us want to know—"Who am I?". We want to know of our worth. We want and need that assurance that what we do makes a difference.

These devotionals are based on three thoughts as Christians. We are:

⚓accepted

⚓secure

⚓significant

Let these devotionals not only spark information to your brain, but may the time you spend with God cause you to realize your worth in Him!

Anchor Notes

Who am I?

Think about the following statement:

I am complete in Christ,
therefore I am accepted!

What does that statement say to you personally?

_____

_____

How does that statement make you feel?

_____

_____

Is that statement true? Why? Why not?

_____

Check out Colossians 2:10.
What do you think it means to be "complete" in Christ?

_____

Who has "accepted" you by this statement?

_____

What did you do to be "accepted"?

___

What do you do in order to be "accepted" by those you are around?

___

If you were living out that statement—how would your life be different?

___

The words to a popular youth camp song say:

> *"I am somebody, because God loves me. I'm accepted, just the way that I am.*
> *His love is higher. It's deeper and wider.*
> *Than you or I will ever understand."*

If we could come to the point where we sing this song and believe it, we should have such a better understanding of "who" we are and "how" to anchor our hope in worth!

Inspirational Stories and Devotionals

Who am I?

Who are some people that are considered "acceptable" in the world today.

___

What makes them "acceptable"?

___

Ponder this statement:

I am God's child, therefore I am accepted!

How does that statement make you feel?

___

Check out—John 1:12 -
Think of *one* word that describes that verse:

___

If you lived in a castle and your dad was the king, what do you think your childhood would have been like?

___

As Christians, we are all children of God—King's Kids. All of us accepted by the very one who made us. All in God's family.

Anchors of Hope

Who do you know that is not part of God's family? All has never called to God and asked for that everlasting acceptance?

_____

_____

Will you recognize who you are in Christ? Will you recognize the Anchor of Worth that you are to Him? Spend some time praying for the people that don't know Jesus as their personal friend and Savior.

On your "Anchor Notes" page, plan out a way that you can begin to share Christ with those who don't know Him!

Ask God to lead you—He wants them most of all in the family!

⚓ Anchor Notes

_____

_____

_____

_____

_____

_____

_____

Inspirational Stories and Devotionals

Who am I?

> To begin this devotional—please take a minute and make a prayer list. Use the Anchor notes page. Include on your list, those people that you need to be standing in the gap for in prayer. Also, list those things in which you are need. Spend some important time with God.

Think about this:

I can find grace and mercy in time of need, therefore I am secure.

What a statement!—How does that make you feel?

_____

_____

Check out Hebrews 4:16.
What does that verse say to you?

_____

_____

As you read the following, picture the scene in your mind.

Visualize yourself coming before God.

What does it look like?

Before you is God Almighty. His angels say, "You may approach the King." As you walk closer to Him, you keep your head down. Because you are in His presence, you can't look up. You need to talk to Him but you feel in awe. He somehow let's you know it's ok to talk, ask questions, or just sit in His presence.

So talk, ask, sit . . .

After a while, you hear Him clearly say -
"You have been given His grace and mercy.
He will always be there for you. Always!"

Approach and anchor with confidence!

⚓ Anchor Notes

Inspirational Stories and Devotionals

Who am I?

Question: What are some things that separate us from other people?

_____

_____

How do you feel when you are separated from folks that you care about?

_____

Do you remember in history when a country's separation wall was broken down? Do you remember the Berlin wall coming down? What kind of emotion did you see from those people?

_____

When I watched the news and saw "the wall of separation" come down it reminded me that God's love has never nor will it ever be behind a wall. Romans 8:35-39. Find it, read it. Make a list of things that can't separate us from God:

_____

_____

Will you believe the following statement?

I cannot be separated from the love of God, therefore I am secure.

How big is "security" to you?

_____

We need to know that some things will always be secure. That we can count on it! For those and many other reasons, I love those verses. They are promises to me that God will never leave me.

On the "Anchor Notes" sheet, draw two footprints. (these represent your feet). Write your name on each print. Pick one of the verses from Romans and write beneath the footprints. Remind yourself that you can stand on the promises of God as you anchor your hope in worth.

 Anchor Notes

Who am I?

Quick question:
   What is the purpose of "salt"?

___

   What is the purpose of "light"?

___

   Why would God call us to be "salt" and "Light"?

___

___

Get your Bible and read Matt. 5:13-14. (Read your Bible first.) Here's the same verse from "The Message" by Eugene Peterson.

"Let me tell you why you are here. You're here to be salt-seasoning that brings out the God-flavors of this earth. If you lose your saltiness, how will people taste godliness? You've loss your usefulness and will end up in the garbage.

Here's another way to put it: You're here to be light, bringing out the God-colors in the world. God is not a secret to be kept. We're going public with this, as public as a city on a hill."

What does it mean to bring out the God-flavors of this earth?

___

What does it mean to bring out the God-colors of this earth?

___

Does it mean that you can lose your salvation if you lose the salt or light?

Some may understand it differently, but I think that Jesus is not talking about our salvation, but our walk with Him. We miss out on so much when we fail to spend time with Him. Doesn't mean that He is throwing us out of the family, however.

Say to yourself:

I am the salt and light of the earth, therefore I am significant.

Inspirational Stories and Devotionals

Who am I?

I am God's workmanship,
therefore I am significant.

> work-man-ship n.
> 1. The skill of a craftsperson or an artisan.
> 2. The quality of something made, as by an artisan.
> 3. Something made or produced by a workman.
> 4. The product of effort or endeavor.
>
> We are God's workmanship. What an incredible thought—each of us!

Read Ephesians 2:10.
What is it that God is making out of your life?

_____

So often we think the question "Who Am I?" is tough to answer.

Now you have six statements that should anchor your hope in your worth. Six statements about who we are in Christ Jesus!

Take a few minutes to go back over the six devotionals in this section. Write down your six promises of worth! (ex. I am complete in Christ, therefore I am accepted.)

_____

_____

_____

Anchors of Hope

_____

_____

On the Anchor Notes sheet, write a prayer of thanks. Remember that we do have anchors of hope!

Anchor Notes

....

....

....

....

....

....

....

....

....

Anchors of Worth

For adopted kids, finding a sense of worth is a tough process. I know it first hand.

My parents adopted my older two brothers and I. They did a tremendous job of sharing with me about being adopted and what it means. I grew up with the knowledge that I was "special" and "chosen."

When I was 7 years old, I was in my little class at church. Our teacher was teaching us about being a Christian. She said that being a Christian meant that you were adopted into His family. Knowing that I was adopted, my teacher asked me to share with the class what it meant to be adopted. I quickly and proudly shared that it meant that you were "special" and "chosen". As she continued to explain the process, I realized that I wanted to be adopted in God's family as well. Being part of God's family would certainly give me worth. I have misunderstood lots information concerning God in my lifetime, but being worth something in His family is certainly information I wanted and understood.

For an adopted kid, to be worth something to God was vital. It was significant in finding worth. It was an anchor of worth by the very fact that I was part of God's family. I had worth. Worth that couldn't be destroyed or taken away.

I remember after becoming a Christian that my prayer at night was quite simple. It went something like this, "I love you God." Nothing fancy. I knew He found worth in me and I loved Him for that. As I got older, I thought fancier, longer prayers were what God really wanted to hear. When I became a parent, I realized that my first prayer was probably the best. Because God has given us worth, our love for Him is always "worth" it!

Most of the time we associate worth with "doing". The more a person does, the more he or she is worth. It's an incredible thought because it drives us to just be people that do and do and do . . . It's a vicious cycle.

Though we may think great knowledge always comes in big, huge books—we are wrong! I read a little book by Henry J.M. Nouwen, *The Path of Peace*, which contained big, important knowledge about worth, doing and being. Dr. Nouwen has written lots of books and taught at distinguished universities such as Notre Dame, Yale and Harvard. He spent the last years of his life serving as the pastor of a community of mentally handicapped persons in Toronto, Canada.

In his book, Nouwen shares about those folks in the community and at the house where he worked. One particular 25 year old man named Adam teaches much about our worth. Adam's body didn't allow him to talk, walk, eat by himself, or communicate in most ways. What Adam "did" was definitely not a way to describe Adam's worth. His being there at the house was enough. When Adam was not at the house, his presence was missed. Not that he did anything of what we would consider "worth", but it was his presence that was "worth" everything. Oh that we would learn those lessons! What a classroom experience. Learning about who God wants one to be, by example.

Jesus was the messenger of worth. He brought worth to the sick by way of healing. He brought worth to women by conversation. He brought worth with those He traveled and lived with by example. He brought worth to those who were dead, by providing everlasting life. Jesus elevated people with worth!

> *"And even the very hairs of your head are all numbered. So don't be afraid; you are worth more than many sparrows."*
> *Matthew 10:30-31*

Inspirational Stories and Devotionals

Letters of Hope

Take a minute. Write a prayer. Share a word of thanks to God for your worth!

_____

_____

_____

_____

_____

_____

_____

_____

_____

_____

_____

_____

_____

_____

Anchor Notes

Do you . . . ?
Anchoring Hope with Life

"I sure hope . . . " Ever thought that? Sure we all have. Hope lends itself to action. Actions from ourselves. Actions we see in others.

The following devotionals are going to require you to get up and get items to help you with your time with God. You'll get much more out of these devotionals because of the action you take in doing these devotionals. It would be really easy just to read through these devotionals, but don't sell your time with God short.

Anchor in Action—Do It!

"Therefore, prepare your minds for action; be self-controlled; set your hope fully on the grace to be given you when Jesus Christ is revealed."
1 Peter 1:13

Anchor Notes

Inspirational Stories and Devotionals

Do you . . . ?
"Really Pray for your Friends?"

You'll need for this devotional—several postcards.
Prayer is an incredible thing when you think about it. Communicating with God. Having access to God.
Think for a minute and list five answered prayers:

1. _____

2. _____

3. _____

4. _____

5. _____

What does it mean to pray for a friend?

Have you ever said to someone, "I'll be praying for you" but you forgot? Got busy with your own life and just didn't remember? Sure we all have.

Check out Philemon 4-5.
Wouldn't be great for someone to write you and say that to you?
One way to anchor hope in action is to stand in the gap for others—through prayer. To pray and praise God for a friend.

Who have you told you would remember in prayer?

Pray for them now.
Take the postcard that you have with you and send a note to the person(s) for which you just prayed. Imagine how he or she will feel—perhaps much like Philemon.

Anchor Notes

Do you . . . ?
"Let your Fingers do the Walking"

You'll need your local telephone book along with your Bible for this devotional.

Take out the phone book and look through it. Check out all the "other" stuff in it besides phone numbers.

What extra information did you find?

_____

_____

So much information besides just phone numbers! Read 2 Timothy 3:14-17.

Question—How are the phone book and the Bible similar? (ex. lots of helpful info./more than expected, etc.)

_____

_____

What is Paul trying to teach Timothy in these verses?

_____

_____

What is God trying to teach you in these verses?

_____

_____

There is so much more—the Bible is full of new information each time we read it. It not only provides the history of the past, it provides the teaching for tomorrow. It's the light of our very existence. Let your fingers and heart walk daily in God's word!

Do you . . . ?
"Hide it Under a Bush"

You'll need some balloons, markers, and a pin(straight) for this devotional.

Read Romans 12:1-12. As you read these verses, take the balloons—blow them up, using a marker, write one gift on each balloon.

Take a minute and look at all the balloons—look at all the gifts that God gives.

Shuffle the balloons around. Pick one up—look at the gift. Do you know of someone (including yourself) that might have that gift. Write their name(s) on the balloon. Continue until you have names on all the balloons.

Say a prayer of thanks for these gifts and these people of whom have these gifts—but don't close your eyes.

Take the pin and pop one of the balloons—the one with your name on it.

How did you feel?

_____

How do you think God feels when we don't use the gifts He has given to us?

_____

What do we do to the other balloons/people when we are not using our gift(s)?

_____

Not using what God has given us is not what was or is intended! We are to use the gifts that we have to give God glory. Using these gifts, gives us anchors of action—anchors of hope.

Inspirational Stories and Devotionals

Do you...?
"Give Kisses and Hugs"

You'll need some Hershey's Kisses and Hugs® for this devotional.
This ought to be a fun devotional for you chocolate lovers! For those of you on diets—sorry!
During the months of May and June there are two important celebrated days—remember what they are?

If we have a special day for Mother's Day and another special day for Father's Day, when is kids' day? Trick question—everyday!
Check out Ephesians 6:1—4.
Those verses are full of how we should respect and love our parents.
How do you or did you show respect for your parents?

As children, we were more open to hugging and kissing our parents. What parent doesn't want and waits with anticipation to have their child say I love you for the first time? But as a teenager or adult, we come to a point where we think it isn't cool to kiss or hug our parent(s). That doesn't mean that we have to stop sharing our love with them.
We call God—Father because He takes us as His child. He loves us like His child. He calls us His child.
Now—(I hope you haven't eaten all your chocolate) take a Hershey's kiss or hug and put it in your mouth. Let it remind you of God's love for you.
Find a way to use your "Kisses and Hugs" to share with your parent(s), your child or a friend you care for. Either write a note with the kisses and leave it in a place just for that designated person or hand it to them, tell them you love them.

Do you . . . ?
"Get plenty of Rest"

You'll need to go outside for this devotional. Do it on a pretty day—adds to the meaning!

As you look around you, take a few moments to relax. Enjoy being a part of God's creation!

Read Hebrews 4:1-13.

What do those verses say to you?

___

___

___

What is most appealing about resting with God?

___

___

For the next 15 minutes—simply rest!

What did you learn about resting?

___

What was the hardest things about resting?

___

How could you convince a friend to rest with the experience that you just had?

___

___

Do you . . . ?
"Wanna be Rich"

For this devotional you'll need some money—dollars and coins.

Take your money out and answer the following questions:

1. How hard was it for you to make the money at which you're looking?

2. What will you do with that money?

3. What did you sacrifice in order to get that money?

If I were to tell you that I had a "Secret Treasure Map" that if you could figure it out, you'd be rich—all you have to do is write and ask for a copy of the map—would you?

Some would—some wouldn't. If you knew how much the "treasure" was worth—would that play a part in your decision?

Read 1 Timothy 6:3-10.

What does Paul mean in verse 6—"godliness with contentment is great gain?"

In the Bible version, "The Message" verse 6 states this: "A devout life does bring wealth, but it's the rich simplicity of being yourself before God."

Read that again. What does that verse say to you?

We are so rich in Christ. We don't need a treasure map to find riches—we just need His eyes to know of all the neat riches we have around us. If you have those—you are rich!

 # Anchor Notes

Anchors of Action

A verb is defined in *The American Dictionary* as "that part of speech that expresses action."

How can we anchor in action? How can we not?

Walking, talking, healing, sleeping, eating, praying, teaching, laughing, listening, waiting, touching, preaching,—all actions of Jesus. All actions to anchor our hope within. All actions that made a difference—then and now!

We learn from an early age that actions speak louder than words. This certainly has some truth to it. Actions live out lots of words. Take for instant, the time when Jesus was speaking and healing and the number of people there were about five thousand men, not counting women and children. Jesus certainly could have said to the disciples that He was tired and had done all that he could do. It wasn't His fault that there were that many people and it had gone that long. How was He supposed to know to tell the people to bring their meal with them? He had been active in meeting their needs!

But Jesus knew that His actions would always anchor another life. Feeding the sheep was not just spiritual, but physical. Instead of listening to Jesus share with the people words about going home and eating, He let His actions speak. His actions anchored each hungry person. His actions were an example of what He taught. His actions went beyond His teaching.

Jesus replied, "They do not need to go away. You give them something to eat." "We have here only five loaves of bread and two fish," they answered. "Bring them here to me," he said. And he directed the people to sit down on the grass. Taking the five loaves and the two fish and looking up to heaven, he gave thanks and broke the loaves. Then he gave them to the disciples, and the disci-

ples gave them to the people. They all ate and were satisfied, and the disciples picked up twelve basketfuls of broken pieces that were left over."
Matthew 14:16-20

People who set that kind of example of modeling are like what I've heard called, "Jesus with skin." People who let the actions of Jesus lead their lives. I recently heard about a women whose church recognized her for 48 years of teaching in a Sunday School class. She is a "Jesus with Skin." How many actions went unnoticed? How many lives did she touch? She must have taught story after story from the Bible. The difference she made was the action with which she lived out those stories.

I found the following poem in the book, *Molder of Dream* by Guy Rice Doud. Mr. Doud was National Teacher of the Year and the book is about his journey. The poem comes from "Collected Verse of Edgar A Guest". It describes— anchors of action!

"Sermons We See"

I'd rather see a sermon than hear one any day;
I'd rather you walk with me than merely tell the way.
The eye's a better pupil and more willing than the ear,
Fine counsel is confusing, but example's always clear.

Letters of Hope

Take a minute. Write a prayer. Ask God to show you how to be an example of action!

_____

_____

_____

_____

_____

_____

_____

_____

_____

_____

_____

_____

_____

_____

Anchor Notes

Ways to Encourage
Anchoring Hope through Courage

Encouragement rarely comes only in one form or from one source. We get encouraged from different things and in different ways!

The Bible is full of encouragement. These Bible studies will challenge you to examine encouragement through a scripture passage, specific words, a person, an act, a place and a story. The devotionals don't begin to exhaust all the many ways that encouragement is found in the Bible.

It takes both courage to give encouragement and courage to receive encouragement. We are great at playing off compliments and words of encouragement. Yet, Christ taught us to lift one another up. To cheer for and support each other.

"But Christ is faithful as a son over God's house. And we are his house, if we hold on to our courage and the hope of which we boast."
Hebrews 4:6

"May the God who gives endurance and encouragement give you a spirit of unity among yourselves as you follow Christ Jesus, so that with one heart and mouth you may glorify the God and Father of our Lord Jesus Christ."
Romans 15:5-6

Anchor Notes

A Passage to Encourage!

As you think about this past week, what has been a high moment?

What has been a low moment?

Honestly, which was easiest to remember?

We teach that for every criticism we hear, we must hear seven positive statements to off-set that criticism. In other words we are more likely to remember criticism, even if it's a little, rather than lots of praise. Why?

Check out this special passage of encouragement found in Matthew 11:28-30.

What does this passage say to you?

How could this passage encourage you this week?

There is a legend that states that birds did not have wings at first. When the birds were given wings, they rebelled. The wings were a burden to the birds. When the birds began to accept the wings, these burdens lifted them to the sky.

If you read the passage, you notice that Christ wore a yoke. The weight of Christ's yoke is the wings to the soul.

One commentary stated that Christ's yoke should have had the following inscribed on it:

Deus Vult—Latin for "God wants or wishes."

God wants us to learn *from* Jesus—not about Jesus!

What a passage of encouragement!

What an incredible God!

Anchor Notes

A Word to Encourage!

Words are so important. We use them freely, yet there are some that are precious to us. Besides your name, list words that you love for someone to say to you:

_____

_____

_____

What is or was important about those words?

_____

The Bible is full of incredible words. Words such as hope, love, salvation, peace, etc. The word of encouragement I want you to think about during these next few moments is that incredible word—GRACE—Webster defines it this way:

1. Seemingly effortless beauty or charm of movement, form, or proportion.
2. A characteristic or quality pleasing for its charm or refinement.
3. A sense of fitness or propriety.
4. a. A disposition to be generous or helpful; goodwill. b. Mercy; clemency.
5. A favor rendered by one who need not do so; indulgence.
6. A temporary immunity or exemption; a reprieve.

How do you define "grace"?

_____

However we define it—God provides enough in any situation.

Look at 2 Corinthians 12:9.

Paul would certainly know how it feels to have a bad day. He would be one that could say, "know how that feels!" He begged God to take away the thorn in his flesh. And when God didn't, he realized that because of this thing called grace—he had something given to him that his thorn couldn't touch.

How about you?

It's a Word to Encourage!

 # Anchor Notes

A Person to Encourage!

As you begin this devotional, take a minute to list the friends you know that are "Never give up" type of people.

_____

_____

Say a special prayer of thanks for them!
The Bible is full of people that encourage us as Christians. Who are some of your favorites?

_____

What do you think is in the make-up of these "never give up" type people?

_____

Remember with me in Matthew 28:1-10 and the ladies that went to the tomb.
Do you think that these ladies knew that what they were doing was extra-ordinary, beyond what was required, giving more of themselves that morning?

_____

Probably not!
People who never give—are like that! They usually don't think about what it cost them to get something done, they are just willing to go that second mile. They are willing to be the ordinary, doing the extra-ordinary!
How about you?
Will you strive this day to be a person to encourage?

Anchors of Hope

Not giving up on people, projects, situations? How will you accomplish this?

_____

_____

Anchor Notes

An Act to Encourage!

Quick—stand up and state the Bible's shortest verse - Remember it, sure you do, it's John 11:35. (thought I was going to tell you didn't you!)

If you were interviewed on a television show, and the interviewer asked you the following question, how would you respond?

What is an act of an encourager?

_____

_____

(For those of you with the dramatic flair, hold your pencil up to your mouth and pretend you are actually answering the reporter!)

As I thought about the act of an encourager, one thought stuck out in my mind—an act that is real. In John 11:35, Jesus does one of the most real things in life. He cries. The Almighty demonstrates that He knows pain—and as one writer puts it, "pain is universal."

Question—How does Jesus acknowledging pain (by weeping) make Him an encourager to you?

_____

_____

Think about it—if someone were to say, describe Jesus, would you say—He cared for the uncared for, he taught with passion, he cried? Doubt it, but as an act of encouragement, He did show this intense emotion with others. Who has cried with you in a difficult situation?

Anchors of Hope

Was it hard to remember their name, probably not. We don't forget people that stick beside us in that way, do we?

It's an Act of Encouragement!

Anchor Notes

_____

_____

_____

_____

_____

_____

_____

_____

_____

_____

_____

_____

Inspirational Stories and Devotionals

A Place to Encourage!

Where do you go when you need to find a place of Encouragement? Is it someone's house? A special room in your house? A place where you've felt especially close to God in the past?

_____

What do you take with you when you go to this special place?

_____

In Luke, after Jesus died and resurrected, there is a special time and place where some folks probably never forgot. Read Luke 24:13-35

How could the road to Emmaus be a place of encouragement?

_____

_____

Have you ever had a "road to Emmaus"? What made it that way?

_____

The key to the Emmaus road was this fact:

Jesus was there!

Ever been on a road—just going through life and felt like Jesus was there. He was there traveling with you. He was sharing the same road?

If Jesus traveled that day with those folks on the

Emmaus road, will He travel with you?

Yes, He can and He will! So, when you think you're heading through your journey alone, remember that there will always be a traveler with you. Cheering for you. Waiting to encourage you in His hope!

What a Way and Place to Encourage!

Anchor Notes

A Story to Encourage!

Because in each of us, there has been a story of encouragement. A special time or place where someone has reached out in a special way and we have received their encouragement.

During this devotional I want you to think of that time. Let this encouragement warm your heart again.

On the next page, try to write out what happened in your story of encouragement.

- Think about what that person did special for you.

- Think about how you felt. Was it easy to accept their encouragement?

- How did you see Jesus in that person or in the act of encouragement?

Your Story to Encouragement

by _____

_____

_____

_____

_____

_____

Anchors of Hope

There are many "Ways of Encouragement". As you have now penned this one experience, may you see the importance of letting others know of encouragement through "Stories to Encouragement."

Anchor Notes

Anchors of Support

Ever have something exciting happen in your life that made you numb—completely head to toe numb? It's a weird feeling. When people show and demonstrate that anchor of support, the exciting feeling that comes with that is amazing.

I remember everything about that moment, except what clothes I had on. Sitting at my desk, working. Trying to get lots of last minute things done on several ministry projects, when the phone rings. The secretaries were gone, so I answered it generically and found the call for me.

It was Rick Lawrence, editor of *Group* magazine. He had called some months earlier informing me about a special recognition in their youth ministry magazine called, "Youth Leader of the Year." We talked and I shared information concerning the youth ministry that I lead. Afterwards, I concluded that it must have been a lean year on nominee's for I was in the top 10 of their pick.

When I picked up the phone this time and realized this guy was now calling again, I thought, how nice, Rick calls back those who don't get picked—how sweet! But that was not the message of the call. He was calling to share of my selection as "Youth Leader of the Year." For those of you who don't work with teenagers we get complaints—pretty often. Grips—all the time. But an award—what is that?

When I finally decided that the call was not a joke, and that what he stated was truth—the numbness began. I had never had that happen before. I sat completely numb. Pinch me, I'm dreaming. When I could finally stand, I don't believe that I touched the ground.

Being tapped as "Youth Leader of the Year" didn't mean our ministry was the best—it just meant to me that some of the things we were doing were on track. The youth ministry team actually should have received the award. You are only as effective as the team you have around you.

The anchor of support had begun. The demonstration of what it means to go the extra mile—to support beyond, I was about to learn first hand. As part of their award, I received a nice plaque. I got to attend this great conference. All the words of praise and encouragement were humbling. But, the greatest anchor of support was what happened throughout the next year. The magazine staff, during staff meetings, would sign a card to me. Each person, some I knew most I did not, would write and encourage me. Their words of thanks seemed like million dollar gifts. It was such an incredible anchor of support.

Not long after receiving that award, I had the chance to begin a ministry much like what I had received from the cards of support. Anchor Ministries, Inc. is a direct result of God's leadership and others who supported and encouraged me.

When you become an anchor of support, the difference you make usually gets passed on to someone else as support. Then to another, and so on and so on! Because *Group* chose to support me, God directed me to support others. The 10 cards I received from the magazine staff became anchors of support. In the time that I've ministered through Anchor Ministries (since May 1994), we have sent over 7,000 individual letters of support to others. The anchor continues.

To demonstrate God's support, His everlasting Anchor, He supported us with His life and His death. All of who Jesus Christ is can anchor our lives in support. The apostle Paul shares about that support and love that Jesus demonstrated.

"You see, at just the right time, when we were still powerless, Christ died for the ungodly. Very rarely will anyone die for a righteous man, though for a good man someone might possibley dare to die. But God demonstrates his own love for us in this; While we were still sinners, Christ died for us."
Romans 5:6-8

Inspirational Stories and Devotionals

Letters of Hope

Take a minute. Write a prayer. Share a word of thanks to God for the ways others support and encourage you!

_____

_____

_____

_____

_____

_____

_____

_____

_____

_____

_____

_____

_____

_____

Anchor Notes

Risks
Anchoring Hope on the Edge

"Risks—Life on the Edge."—Are you sure that you want to go down this path? Are you sure you want to do these devotionals?

The Bible never promises that when a person accepts Christ they live in a plastic bubble. A plastic bubble that protects a person from any harm, hurt, disappointment, or heartache. Christian or non-Christian, we still live in the world.

How many risks have you taken today?

Life is full of them! It would be hard to call it life without the word "risk".

As you do these devotionals, risk something. Remember that we are anchoring hope on the edge. The edge or risk in not ours alone! There is hope because of the security Christ alone provides.

"I can do everything through him

who gives me strength."

Philippians 4:13

Anchor Notes

Risks

What is your definition of the word "risk"?

What makes that definition different from the word "decision"?

One definition for the word *risk* :
2. A factor, thing, element, or course involving uncertain danger; a hazard.

One definition for the word *decision*:
1. The passing of judgment on an issue under consideration.

Others have defined risk as living life on the edge.

Helen Keller stated, "Life is either a daring adventure or nothing." I think that decisions and risks are much alike, however, there are some major differences!

Think about today—what decisions do you need to make?

What risk will they have?

Do you risk letting people know who you really are?

Do you risk sharing what you know with others?

Thomas Fuller says, "Security is the mother of danger and the grandmother of destruction."

Pray that God will teach you how to risk! Today

Anchors of Hope

Risks

Begin your devotional with prayer—Ask God to open your heart and take the risk to change!

Turn in your Bible to Hebrews 11:1-16.

We know these scriptures as the family album of faith. Those who have taken the risk to change who they were and become people of faith.

As you read about these folks, do you get the idea that they were just automatically like that—faith people?

What happened that each one of them took on the very essence of faith?

You're apart of the family album!

Think about the following questions.

1. Look at the way verse 5 begins, verse 7, verse 8, verse 20, verse 21, verse 22.

2. After thinking about your life and the challenges and changes you've made—even if they may not appear to society as some big change—change is change—bring the family album up to date to include you! Finish the following verse:

By faith _____(your name), _____

_____

_____

_____

_____

Oh to risk it all to be in that Family Album of Faith!

Risks

I.D. Thomas, in *A Word from the Wise*, tells the story of a Georgia farmer living in a dilapidated shack. He hadn't planted anything, so nothing needed to be cultivated. The farmer just sat, ragged and barefoot, surrounded by the evidence of his laziness.

A stranger stopped for a drink of water and asked, "How's your cotton doing?"

"Ain't got none," replied the farmer.

"Didn't you plant any?"

"Nope. 'fraid of boll weevils."

Well," continued the visitor, "how's your corn?"

"Didn't plant none. 'fraid there wasn't gonna be no rain."

"How are your potatoes?"

"Ain't got none. Scared of potato bugs."

"Really? What did you plant?"

"Nothin'," was the reply. "I just played it safe."

What area in your life are you most likely to play it safe? Why?

Playing it safe isn't always bad, but never risking anything can make you lazy. Proverbs has some tough things to say about that—check out Proverbs 12:24, 27; 15:19; 18:9.

Pretty tough verses.

Now check out Matthew 25:14-30. What do those verses state about risk?

Who did risk in these verses?

Remember, that yes the first two servants did risk, but the Man taking the journey did risk as well.

Seek God and discover which of the servants you are most like.

Why are you like that particular one?

Do you want to be like any of the other servants?

"Don't be afraid to go out on a limb. That's where the fruit is."
—Arthur F. Lenehan

Anchor Notes

Risks

"Our Example"
One of the first responses of a child is to imitate what he/she sees. Adults get in their tiny little faces and make complete fools of ourselves just to get this response out of the child. I can say this—I've done it!

The greatest example of flattery is imitation. As Christians, that's really what we're called to do—imitate Christ. Do what He has called and been the example to do.

All this to say, God does take risks—that's for all you guys that say, No way am I going to get out on a limb!

Check out Luke 15:1-7.

Quick—how many sermons have you heard on those scriptures?

Many, probably, but have you ever thought about verse 4. The New International Version Bible says, "Does he not leave the ninety-nine in the open country and . . ."

Was that risky? to leave the 99 out in the open?
Who did he leave in charge?
What risk was it to him?
What risk was it to the other sheep?
Plenty—but he risked it all!

God says to me—risk is tough. There are times when you may risk it all—but just remember—You won't go through something I hadn't been through before—there is a path!

How about you?

Anchor Notes

Risks

Some of you know that I do lots of writing out on a boat. As I was preparing for these devotionals, it was the most incredible day—especially out on a boat! The lake calmly states "peace".

Just thinking about the word "risk"—I think of chaos—things all around—pressure—etc.

List the people that you're needing to take a risk with:

_____

_____

List the decisions that will cause you to risk:

_____

_____

List the situations that cause you risk:

_____

Take your Bible, this devotional and find a special place to pray over the risks in your life.

"For God is not a God of disorder but of peace."
1 Corinthians 14:33

Anchors of Hope

In other words, don't make risky decisions where there is disorder—get away and find a place of Peace—God is the God of Peace.

At your peaceful place, what risks are you willing to take?

_____

_____

Taking a risk is hard enough—don't forget to find a place to go in order to sort out all parts of the risk before making a decision.

The lake helped me today—find peace among living life on the edge—there's no better way to live!

Risks

Finally—the last devotional on risks!
Think back through the Bible—jot down people in the Bible that took a risk

Name   Risk

_____

_____

_____

_____

These ordinary people—like you and me—took risks. Big risks—for Christ.

C.S. Lewis once stated, "Courage is not simply one of the virtues, but the form of every virtue at the testing point."

Jesus said, "And surely I am with you, always, to the very end of the age."

Take the risk—you are not alone!!

Before Helen Keller said, "Life is either a daring adventure or nothing, she said Security is mostly a superstition. It does not exist in nature, nor do the children of men as a whole experience it. Avoiding danger is no safer in the long run than outright adventure.

Being a Christian is "the great Adventure!" Taking risks for Christ. Living on the edge of helping others. Getting out of our comfort zone in order to break through this world with the Good News!

What a better risk—with heavenly rewards!
Take the risk!

Letters of Hope

Take a minute. Write a prayer. Share a word of thanks to God because risks are safe with Him!

_____

_____

_____

_____

_____

_____

_____

_____

_____

_____

_____

_____

_____

_____

Anchors of Security

Security—one minute you have it, another minute you don't. And when you don't, that's an incredible feeling. That feeling of sudden loss. That gut feeling of being physically hit, but knowing the person that hit you is not around. It's like looking in a well with no bottom and realizing that you've just dropped something incredibly precious. Where is my child? Where is my mate? What happened to my job?

People experience the risks of this world hundreds of times a day. Children snatched from their parents. Spouses that leave for work and never return home. People who invest their time and energy in a company only to find their "pink" slip on their chair after lunch. Forever their lives changed. Life is so risky. Where is security? Is it possible in this world?

My son loves riding the bus home from school. In second grade, it's still fun. He's with all his friends talking, laughing, and being a kid. It's nice to know some things in life haven't changed. But when the bus came, and Alan didn't come home, the risks of this world began to surround and sing a horrible tune to me. In the next hour of fear, I realized how risky it is in this world.

So many things go through your head when you think a risk has turned bad. Questions without immediate answers. Answers without sensible questions. It happens to us all because risks are everywhere!

Jesus knew much about the word "risk". In the tenth chapter of the book of John, He discussed the risk of believing and following Him to some fellow Jews. They were so scared to really believe that He was the Christ. The risk was too great for them. Jesus promised that the risk would be worth it:

"My sheep listen to my voice; I know them, and they follow me. I give them eternal life, and they shall never perish; no one can snatch them out of my hand. My Father, who has given them to me, is greater than all; no one can snatch them out of my Father's hand. I and the Father are one." (vss. 27-30)

Once we belong to Him, we can anchor to the security of God. That doesn't mean that we will be immune from hurt or pain—related to the risks of this world. It means that the risks we take will be worth it. Worth it because in the end, we are anchored in the security of Christ.

Later as I held Alan, I thought about the risks of this world. I was also reminded of the security of God. Alan nor I were ever out of God's sight. Risk is letting go and depending on those facts to be true—no matter how each of us felt.

By the way, Alan simply fell asleep on the school bus. What a nap to remember!

"For I am convinced that neither death nor life, neither angels nor demons, neither the present nor the future, nor any powers, neither height nor depth, nor anything else in all creation, will be able to separate us from the love of God that is in Christ Jesus our Lord."
Romans 8:38-39

ANCHORS OF HOPE—strength, worth, action, support, and security. All anchors that support us wherever we are in our journey. I pray that this book has been most useful to you in your time alone with God.

This story is about a man who owns his own business in the northeast. Like many others who own their own business, this man works day and night. His business is profitable. After years of hard work, he decides to retire. He thinks he has worked hard enough and it's time for someone else to take over the business. So, he sells his business and does what many retired folks do—head south.

In Florida, the man sees lots of sun. He watches others load up on boats and head out for peaceful times. He has the money, so he decides to buy a boat as well. He gets out on the boat and experiences just the opposite of what his "working" life provided. He finds peace and quiet. He loves it.

He goes through storms while out in the ocean, but one day a big storm began to scare him. The radio on his boat announces that a hurricane warning is in effect. He realizes his limitations and decides to head back to the dock. At the dock, he finds all the rope he has and ties to everything that doesn't move. While tying to the dock, he notices a Floridian leaning against the post at the dock. The Floridian had obviously lived through these types of storms. As he looked at the man, the Floridian just shook his head slowly—no.

Immediately he checks the ropes again. "Surely I've just missed a rope or something's come untied," he thinks. But as he checks his boat, he finds nothing. Looking back at the man still leaning, he notices that the man has still not stopping shaking his head. "Perhaps I should go over and check out why this man is shaking his head no," he thinks. "Yes, I know what I paid for this boat. I will." And he does.

"Sir, I know that there is a hurricane coming. I've tied everything down that I know how to tie. I look over here and you simply shake your head no. Please explain to me why."

The message of the Floridian is to all of us. "It's not what you tie too, it's what you anchor too!"

Anchor your hope in the cross of Jesus Christ!

Continue this journey!

Anchors of Hope is part of a unique encouragement ministry called Anchor Ministries, Inc. This ministry is a non-profit organization designed to support people on an individual and monthly basis.

In Anchor Ministries, each participant receives each month, devotionals typical of the ones in this book. These devotional are life oriented. Also, during the month, every participant in Anchor Ministries receives a personal letter of encouragement and support from Debbie.

Being part of this ministry means that you are willing to let others minister to your needs. Do you know of someone that might need this type of continual ministry? How about a teenager, college student, minister, or you?

Fill out the following information:

```
Name _____

Address _____

City, State, Zip _____

Phone _____

         Circle the category that best describes you:

                        teenager

                     college student

                  youth leader/minister

                         adult
```

Send this along with your suggested $30.00 donation to:

Anchor Ministries, Inc.
108 Buckingham Ct.
Goodlettsville, Tn. 37072

DEBBIE HARNED is president of Anchor Ministries, Inc., a nonprofit organization striving to support, encourage and minister to others. Debbie is also highly sought after as a speaker and seminar leader. To find out more about Anchor or for more information regarding seminars, specialized materials for youth camps, or speaking engagements, write to:

Anchor Ministries, Inc.
108 Buckingham Ct.
Goodlettsville, Tn. 37072-2146
(615)859-0682
or email address:
AnchorDeep@aol.com